REGIONS OF THE U.S.A.

The Northeast

by Rebecca Felix

PUBLISHED BY THE CHILD'S WORLD ®

The Child's World

Published by The Child's World®
1980 Lookout Drive • Mankato, MN 56003-1705
800-599-READ • www.childsworld.com

Acknowledgments
The Child's World®: Mary Berendes, Publishing Director
Red Line Editorial: Editorial direction
The Design Lab: Design
Amnet: Production
Design Element: Dreamstime

Photographs ©: iStockphoto/Thinkstock, title, 3, 7, 8, 17, 21, 24, 25, 28;
Stockbyte/Thinkstock, title; Photodisc, title, 3; Comstock/Thinkstock, 4;
Red Line Editorial, Inc., 5, 6; Photodisc/Thinkstock, 9; Dorling Kindersley/
Thinkstock, 11; Photos.com/Thinkstock, 12, 22; Shutterstock Images, 14,
15, 23; Hemera/Thinkstock, 19; Jeffrey M. Frank/Shutterstock Images,
20, 31; Lijuan Guo/Shutterstock Images, 26; Stockbyte, 27; Christopher
Penler/Shutterstock Images, 29

Front cover: iStockphoto/Thinkstock; Stockbyte/Thinkstock; Photodisc

ISBN: 978-1623234928
LCCN: 2013931428

Printed in the United States of America
Mankato, MN
July, 2013
PA02170

ABOUT THE AUTHOR

Rebecca Felix is a writer and editor who grew up in the Midwest. She received a bachelor's degree in English from the University of Minnesota, which is her home state. She has edited and written several children's books and currently lives in Florida, which is in the Southeastern region of the United States.

Table of Contents

CHAPTER 1   Rocky Beaches, Rolling Mountains, and Stormy Winters   **4**

CHAPTER 2   Colonies, Immigration, and Revolution   **10**

CHAPTER 3   Liberal Spirit, Seafood, and Syrup   **16**

CHAPTER 4   Melting Pot and Diverse Dishes   **22**

Recipe   27

Fast Facts   28

Glossary   30

Learn More   31

Index   32

CHAPTER ONE

Rocky Beaches, Rolling Mountains, and Stormy Winters

Many of the states in the Northeast border the Atlantic Ocean.

Waves hit rocky shores. Forests and farmland cover rolling hillside. Mountains stretch for miles. This region of the United States is called the Northeast. There are eleven states in the Northeast. Connecticut, Maine, Massachusetts, New Hampshire, Rhode Island, and Vermont

make up the eastern part. They are called the New England states. Delaware, New Jersey, New York, Maryland, and Pennsylvania make up the western part. These states are called the Mid-Atlantic states.

Some of the largest U.S. cities are in the Northeast. These cities include New York City, New York, and Boston, Massachusetts. The first U.S. colonies were established in this region. It has an interesting mix of people and cultures. Its geography is also diverse.

Eleven states make up the Northeast.

Geography

Canada and two Great Lakes make up the northern border. Much of the land here is low, rolling hillside. It is well suited for farmland and orchards. The Adirondack and the Allegheny Mountains are two small ranges in the north.

The Atlantic Ocean makes up the eastern border. Off the coast are several bays. Many port cities are located in these bays or on major rivers. Port cities are places where goods are easily shipped and received. There are also many islands

Montpelier★
Concord ★
★Augusta
Albany★
★Boston
Hartford ★
★Providence
Harrisburg★
★Trenton
★Dover
★Annapolis

Hurricane Sandy in 2012 was almost 1,000 miles (1,600 km) wide. It caused billions of dollars of damage in the Northeast.

off the coast. These islands include Cape Cod and Martha's Vineyard. New York City also includes many small islands.

Land along the ocean is mainly flat. It is called the Atlantic coastal plain. West of the coastal plains are the Appalachian Mountains. They run the length of the Northeast. The range is millions of years old. The tops of the mountains are round. Rain and wind wore them down over the years.

The Allegheny River and the Potomac River are west of the Appalachian Mountains. Eastern rivers include the Hudson River and the Connecticut River.

The Northeast has many forests with pine and fir trees. There are also many **deciduous** trees. These include beech, oak, and maple trees. Deciduous tree leaves turn bright colors in fall. Many people travel to the Northeast to see the colorful forests.

Climate

The Northeast has four seasons. Being near the ocean **regulates** temperatures in the area. But the ocean can bring extreme weather, too. It is hurricane season from summer to fall. Hurricanes bring strong winds and flooding. Another ocean storm develops in winter. Strong eastern winds blow in heavy rain, snow, and giant waves. These storms are called Nor'easters. Their winds can be stronger than hurricane winds.

Wildlife

Many types of animals live in the Northeast. Black bear and moose roam New Hampshire, New York, and Maine. Off the coast of Maine there are crab and lobster. Whales, salmon,

Many bat species live in the Northeast. But millions recently died from a disease caused by a fungus.

White-tailed deer live in parts of the Northeast.

NORTHEAST CAPITALS

American author Mark Twain lived in Connecticut's capital, Hartford, for many years. Delaware became the first state by signing the Constitution December 7, 1787, in Dover. Augusta, Maine, is the easternmost U.S. capital. Annapolis, Maryland, was the country's first National Historic Landmark District. Boston, Massachusetts, was home to the first U.S. college. Concord, New Hampshire, is located on the Merrimack River. Trenton, New Jersey, is on the Delaware River. Toilet paper was invented in Albany, New York. The chocolate capital of the world is right outside Harrisburg, Pennsylvania. Providence, Rhode Island, is the capital of the smallest state. But Montpelier, Vermont, is the United States' smallest capital.

and other sea creatures also swim near the Northeast. Eastern bluebirds and white-tailed deer are found throughout the region. A rare herd of wild horses lives near the western border of Maryland.

CHAPTER TWO

Colonies, Immigration, and Revolution

Paleo-Indians came to North America thousands of years ago. Native American tribes are Paleo-Indian descendants. Languages and customs varied between tribes. Iroquois tribes included the Cayuga, Mohawk, Oneida, Onondaga, and Seneca. These tribes made up the Iroquois Confederacy.

Creation of Colonies

Europeans began colonizing the East Coast in the late 1500s and early 1600s. Thirteen colonies were established on

Many Iroquois died from European diseases. The Iroquois tribe members often lived close together, which helped the diseases spread.

Colonists relied on the help of Native Americans to survive.

the Atlantic coast. These colonies eventually became the first states of the United States. Nine of these colonies were in the Northeast.

Colonists relied on farming, fishing, and trade for survival. They often traded with Native Americans. Contact with colonists exposed Native Americans to new diseases, such as smallpox. Native Americans did not have cures for these diseases, and many died.

Wars

Colonists began to claim more land. Native Americans in the Northeast became **displaced**. This led to King Philip's War from 1675 to 1676.

Fighting for control of the land also led to the French and Indian War between British and French colonists. The war lasted from 1754 to 1763. The British took control of a large portion of French land east of the Mississippi River.

Colonists in the city of Boston, Massachusetts, became upset over tax laws in 1773. One tax made all tea expensive—all except the tea from East India Company. This forced colonists to buy tea from them. On December 16, 1773, colonists protested this tax. They dumped more than 300 chests of tea into the Boston

The Boston Tea Party was the colonists' way of protesting the tea tax.

Harbor. Great Britain stopped all trade to Boston in return. These events in part led to the American **Revolution** in 1775.

Colonists fought for independence from Great Britain in the American Revolution. The war began in Massachusetts. New Jersey, New York, and Pennsylvania were the sites of many battles.

On July 4, 1776, colonial delegates signed the Declaration of Independence in Philadelphia, Pennsylvania. It stated the United States was independent from Great Britain. The war officially ended in 1783.

On September 17, 1787, colonial delegates signed the United States Constitution in Philadelphia. It outlines the laws of the nation and citizens' rights.

The U.S. Civil War broke out between the states in 1861. The Confederacy was made up of Southern states. The Union was made up of Northern states. The Confederacy wanted to separate from the Union. Slavery was a main issue. Most

Boston survived a major fire in 1872. The fire destroyed more than 700 buildings.

of the states in the Union were free states. Maryland and Delaware had slavery. The war ended after four years. Slavery was **abolished**.

Many European **immigrants** came to the United States in the 1800s and 1900s. Ellis Island in New York became a center of immigration. The Statue of Liberty can be seen from Ellis Island.

Ellis Island in New York, in the foreground, was the center of immigration for many years.

The mid-1800s to the early 1900s was also the time of the Industrial Revolution in the United States. Cities grew. Businesses and buildings were built. Populations grew larger. The agriculture, manufacturing, and transportation industries were booming.

In the 1960s, Ellis Island and the Statue of Liberty became National Landmarks. There is also a museum there today.

BOSTON'S HISTORY

Many historic events in the Northeast took place in Boston. One such event was the Boston Massacre on March 5, 1770. British troops were in Boston to enforce tax laws that had been put in place. This upset colonists. They got into a fight with the soldiers. The soldiers fired their guns. Five colonists were killed. The Boston Tea Party was another historic event. The Freedom Trail in Boston connects 16 historic spots and is a tourist destination today.

Present Day

Today, the Northeast is still a center of immigration. It has a mix of cultures. Many cities that were significant historically are large urban centers today. These cities have busy **economies**. They also contain important national and regional government centers.

CHAPTER THREE

Liberal Spirit, Seafood, and Syrup

The Northeast is a national political center. Historic events created revolution and led to war. These events changed government nationwide. The political atmosphere of the Northeast is thought to be liberal. This means in favor of progress and individual participation in politics and government.

Each state in the Northeast has a similar government structure. State government is divided into three branches. A state governor is the head of the executive branch.

The Massachusetts State Capitol building houses all three branches of the state's government.

The governor is elected. Governors oversee state laws, programs, and policies.

Another branch of state government is the legislative branch. Writing laws is a part of each state legislature's job. Overseeing state budgets is also part of the job. All state legislatures in the Northeast are divided into two chambers, or groups. Sharing the responsibilities is a way to keep power in balance.

A state's judicial branch is responsible for its court systems. State courts take care of many types of cases.

Economy

The Atlantic Ocean has been a large part of the economy in the Northeast since colonial times. Ocean products, trade, and recreation remain important today. Port cities are centers of trade. Goods from around the world are shipped to port cities. They are then sent across the United States. Goods from across the United States get sent to port cities. Then they are shipped around the world.

The Atlantic Ocean influences what industries are important, too. Commercial fishing includes catching lobster, scallops, clams, and many types of fish. Lobsters from Maine are a major **export**. Massachusetts, Connecticut, New Jersey, and New York are major U.S. clam

Approximately 90 percent of American lobster in the United States is caught off Maine's coast.

producers. Farms and orchards produce exports as well. New York and Pennsylvania are top dairy producers. Vermont is the top producer of maple syrup in the United States.

The Northeast also has many industrial exports. Aircraft parts are major exports from Connecticut, Maine, and Maryland. Electronics are made in many states, including Vermont and Massachusetts. New York City is home to the New York Stock Exchange (NYSE). It is a marketplace where people buy and sell stocks. Buying stock in a company means

Lobster traps sit on a dock in Maine. Lobster is a major export for the Northeast.

you own a small part of it. The NYSE is one of the largest stock markets in the world.

Tourism is also important to the economy in the Northeast. Large, urban cities in the Northeast host many visitors. Forests, the ocean coast, and the Appalachian Mountains are also a draw. Millions of tourists visit year-round for outdoor activities.

The Gettysburg Battlefield Memorial is a popular attraction in Pennsylvania.

NEW YORK CITY

New York City is the most populated city in the United States. It is a center of culture, finance, and business. The city has several unique areas. Subregions include Brooklyn, the Bronx, Queens, Manhattan, and Staten Island. Cultural neighborhoods include Little Italy and Chinatown. The city is also a center of art and fashion. Entertainment and tourism are a huge part of the city's culture. In 2011, more than 50 million people visited the city! The Statue of Liberty, Times Square, and Ellis Island are a few famous sites.

There are many cultural and historic attractions in the Northeast. One is Gettysburg. It is an important U.S. Civil War battle site in Pennsylvania. Museums throughout the Northeast boost tourism. The dozens of universities in the region also bring visitors and help the economy.

CHAPTER FOUR

Melting Pot and Diverse Dishes

Immigrants brought their traditions and cultures to the Northeast long ago. The British mainly settled New England. People of many cultures settled the Mid-Atlantic. This part of the region is often called the "melting pot." This blend of cultures and **ethnicities** is especially present in large coastal cities.

Immigrants arrived in the Northeast long ago.

Harvard University was established in 1636.

The Northeast is known for its rich political history. Many people are involved in politics. Voters tend to have liberal views.

Education has also historically been important in the Northeast. Europeans who settled the area valued higher education. The Northeast is home to many of the country's top universities. Harvard University and Wellesley College are in Massachusetts. Yale University is in Connecticut, and Brown University is in Rhode Island.

The Northeast has both rural and urban areas. Business, entertainment, and nightlife are major parts of life in big cities. The woodlands, mountains, and Atlantic Ocean coastal areas of the Northeast provide entertainment and adventure. Popular outdoor activities include hiking, boating, and fishing. Watching and attending professional sports are also a big part of New England culture.

Grand Central Station in New York City is one of many busy transportation hubs in the region.

Sometimes people have misconceptions about a region. They may think all people in a certain region act in a similar way. But they are not all alike. People in bigger Northeast cities are sometimes thought to be rude or always in a hurry. Some Northeasterners might be this way. But certainly not everyone. Like its cultures and natural surroundings, people of the Northeast are all different. Some may be just like you!

Philadelphia was voted the top sports-crazy city in 2012.

Food

The ocean influences cuisine in the Northeast. Seafood dishes are common. These dishes include crab, lobster, shellfish, and cod. Local produce is also found in regional dishes. Cranberries are grown in big bogs in the Northeast. Maple syrup is a natural Northeast treat. Some regional foods are named after the cities or states that developed them. New England clam chowder is a famous soup dish. New York

Clambakes are popular in New England. People gather and bake clams in a large pit on stones.

Crab is found in many dishes in the Northeast.

pizza is a special type of thin pizza. A Philly cheesesteak is a sandwich of sliced meat and melted cheese made famous in Philadelphia. Boston baked beans have special ingredients that can include molasses or maple syrup.

These dishes are a small part of what makes the Northeast special. The Northeast is a melting pot of people and cultures, ocean and mountain, and rich history and modern cities.

Cranberry bogs are found in the Northeast.

RECIPE

BOSTON BAKED BEANS

Ingredients:

2 cups navy beans

1/3 cup molasses

1/3 cup brown sugar

3 tablespoons Dijon mustard

3 cups hot water

1/2 pound bacon, cut into 1-inch pieces

1 1/2 cups chopped onion

Directions:

Place beans in a large pot and cover with water. Soak overnight and drain in the morning. Mix the molasses, brown sugar, and Dijon mustard with 3 cups of hot water. Line the bottom of a slow cooker with half of the bacon. Put half of the drained beans on top. Add the onions. Put the rest of the beans and bacon in. Pour the molasses-water mixture over the beans. Cover and cook in the slow cooker on the low setting for 8 hours. Check the water level after 2 hours and add more if needed. Enjoy!

Fast Facts

Population: 62,562,746 (2012 estimate)

    Most populous state: New York (19,570,261, 2012 estimate)

    Least populous state: Vermont (626,011, 2012 estimate)

Area: 196,287 square miles (508,381 sq km)

Highest temperature: 111 degrees
Fahrenheit (44°C) in Pennsylvania in 1936

Lowest temperature: minus-52 degrees
Fahrenheit (-47°C) in New York in 1979

Largest cities: New York City,
New York; Philadelphia, Pennsylvania;
Baltimore, Maryland; Boston,
Massachusetts

Major sports teams: Boston Celtics (NBA, basketball); Boston Red Sox (MLB, baseball); New England Patriots (NFL, football); New York Knicks (NBA, basketball); New York Yankees (MLB, baseball); Philadelphia Flyers (NHL, hockey); Pittsburgh Steelers (NFL, football)

Glossary

abolished (uh-BAH-lished) When a practice is ended, it is abolished. Slavery was abolished after the U.S. Civil War.

deciduous (di-SIJ-oo-uhs) Deciduous trees lose their leaves in fall. Many people travel to the Northeast to see the brightly colored deciduous leaves in fall.

displaced (dis-PLASED) Someone is displaced when they are moved from their usual place. The many colonists who moved into the Northeast displaced Native Americans.

economy (i-KON-uh-mee) Economy is the system of making, buying, and selling things. The ocean plays a large role in the economy in the Northeast.

ethnicities (eth-NIH-sit-ees) Ethnicities are associations with certain groups of people of the same culture. The Northeast is a melting pot of ethnicities.

export (EK-sport) An export is a product made in one place and sold to another place. Lobster is a key export in Maine.

immigrants (IM-i-gruhnts) Immigrants are people who move from another country. Ellis Island in New York City was a center for immigrants.

regulate (REG-yuh-late) To regulate is to manage or control. The ocean helps to regulate the temperature of Northeast areas.

revolution (rev-uh-LOO-shuhn) A revolution is a big change made by a group of people. The colonists were unhappy being controlled, and started a revolution to become independent.

To Learn More

Books

Peppas, Lynn. *What's in the Northeast?* New York: Crabtree, 2011.

Rau, Dana Meachen. *The Northeast*. New York: Scholastic, 2012.

Stone, Tanya Lee. *Regional Wild America: Unique Animals of the Northeast*. Detroit, MI: Blackbirch Press, 2005.

Web Sites

Visit our Web site for links about the Northeast:

childsworld.com/links

Note to Parents, Teachers, and Librarians: We routinely verify our Web links to make sure they are safe and active sites. So encourage your readers to check them out!

Index

Adirondack Mountains, 6
Albany, 9
Allegheny Mountains, 6
Annapolis, 9
Appalachian Mountains,
    7, 20
Atlantic Ocean, 6, 11, 18,
    23
Augusta, 9

Boston, 5, 9, 12,
    13, 15

Cape Cod, 7
climate, 8
colonies, 5, 10–11, 13
Concord, 9

Declaration of
    Independence, 13
Dover, 9

Ellis Island, 14, 21
exports, 18–19

food, 24–25
Freedom Trail, 15

geography, 6–8
government, 16–18

Harrisburg, 9
Hartford, 9
Hudson River, 7
hurricane, 8

immigrants, 14, 22

Martha's Vineyard, 7
Montpelier, 9

Native American tribes,
    10, 11

port city, 6, 18
Providence, 9

tourism, 20–21
Trenton, 9

universities, 21, 23

war, 11–14